D1527325

where I'm from,

where poems come from

where I'm from,

where poems come from

by

George Ella Lyon

Photographs by
Robert Hoskins

"That is question now;
And then comes answer like an Absey book.
King John, i, 9
Shakespeare

Absey & Company
Spring, Texas

Acknowledgements

The author and publisher wish to thank the editors of the following publications in which these poems originally appeared: Iron Mountain Review ("Where I'm From"), Bloodroot ("Marilynn's Montessori Memo" and "Warning"), Kentucky Poetry Review ("Catechisms"), College English ("Rings"), The Texas Observer ("This Kitchen Floor"), Southern Poetry Review ("The Syrup Bucket Lid"), Across the Bridge ("Invocation"), Sinister Wisdom ("Choice"), Appalachian Heritage ("Looking at a Photograph of My Mother, Age 3"), Appalachian Journal ("Stripped" and "Salvation"), Prairie Schooner ("What Began at the Post Office"), and Mountainside ("Cousin Ella Goes to Texas").

In addition, they would like to thank Andrew Mountain Press ("Rhody" and "Papaw" in Mountain, a chapbook; "Cousin Ella Goes to Town," a broadside, and "Growing Light," a poem-in-a-pamphlet), and Harcourt Brace & Company ("For a Super Soup-Bean Supper" in Food Fight, edited and illustrated by Michael J. Rosen).

Special thanks to Robert for the photos, to Jim Curless for permission to use James H. Roberts' diaries, to Marilyn Spitz for her memo, to Cathy for the map design, to my mother for sharing stories; to Steve, Leatha, Martha, Robert, and Betty for responding to the manuscript; and to all my teachers.

George Ella Lyon

To my writers' group:

Marie
Jan
Martha
Leatha
Ann
& Lou

with love and thanks.

Contents

Other People's Words

Voices

Stories

Where You're From

A Poem of Farewell

Foreward

Imagine that you must travel far to tell people something -- a great story of love and brave deeds, recipes for healing, directions for a spiritual journey. Your message is long and complex, but you have no tape recorder or e-mail, no camcorder or telephone, not even pen, paper, parchment, or papyrus to help you carry it along. You may not know how to read and write anyway. What can you do?

You can make a poem. You can make it in your head, choosing words whose sound and rhythm knit them together more closely than words in everyday speech. This way they are easier to remember. And you can choose words which are full of feeling and paint pictures, which let the listener taste the venison at the victory feast, hear the chainmail rattle or the camel snuffle outside the tent. The right words will keep your message alive. This is why we have poetry.

It wasn't invented to be hard to understand or to belong to a few people only. It was invented to carry crucial things through space and time, to help the mind hold and share the heart's treasure. Poetry is for you. It's <u>in</u> you -- in the rhythm of your heartbeat and your walking, in the music of your talk. This book is to help you see and say that. This book is for the poems in us all.

where i'm from,

where poems come from

where I'm from

I am from clothespins,
from Clorox and carbon-tetrachloride,
I am from the dirt under the back porch.
(Black, glistening,
it tasted like beets.)
I am from the forsythia bush
the Dutch elm
whose long-gone limbs I remember
as if they were my own.

I'm from fudge and eyeglasses,
        from Imogene and Alafair.
I'm from the know-it-alls
        and the pass-it-ons,
from Perk up! and Pipe down!
I'm from He restoreth my soul
        with a cottonball lamb
        and ten verses I can say myself.

I'm from Artemus and Billie's Branch,
fried corn and strong coffee.
From the finger my grandfather lost
        to the auger,
the eye my father shut to keep his sight.

Under my bed was a dress box
spilling old pictures,
a sift of lost faces
to drift beneath my dreams.
I am from those moments--
snapped before I budded --
leaf-fall from the family tree.

3

objects

A good way to begin writing poetry is to focus on objects, things around you, stuff. Pick a piece of the material world that matters to you, whether you love, hate, treasure, or are just intrigued by it. Look at this object as if you'd never seen it before. Explore its textures with your hands. Listen to the sound when you touch it or tap it on a table. What does it smell like? What do you think it would taste like? Then write down every response the object calls forth in you.

It's fine to write in phrases, rather than sentences, and don't worry about whether they make sense or fit together, or create a particular effect. You're not writing a poem at this point; you're making a list. But the process is a little like tapping on the walls of your experience to find the secret panel which swings open into a poem.

Once you've got your list, pick out the line or lines that stand out to you. Do you have more to explore here? Could one of these be the secret panel? Could you begin or end with one of these lines? To find out, keep writing, and don't forget to use your senses. Bring the reader into your experience by letting her travel there through details of taste, sound, smell, sight and touch. Consider the difference between "I love baseball, even the stuff that's not fun" and "I love baseball, even when sweat stings my eyes inside the catcher's mask." The first statement gives us information about how the speaker feels; the second one puts us there.

To help you get started, let's look at a poem I wrote right after my mother-in-law died. The object I focus on belonged to her, and we have it in the coffee-table-made-from-a-display-case in our living room.

After the Funeral

O, that baby boot,
that shoe of ivory felt
you wore when your foot
would have fit in the palm
of my son, your grandson's hand!

Actually, I just want to talk about the first two lines.
How would the effect be different if I had written: "It was
an old white baby shoe"?

For starters, we would be likely to picture the leather
machine-made baby shoes we see on babies today. But the
poem shows us footwear much older than that, from a time
when such shoes were handmade of soft cloth.

The main trouble with "It was an old white baby shoe,"
then, is that it's too general, which for the reader translates
as <u>distant</u>. Imagine a camera with a zoom lens. When you
look through the regular lens, you see "old white baby
shoe," but by using the zoom, you pull us close so we can
see color (<u>ivory</u>), texture (<u>felt</u>) and design (<u>boot</u>).

You may have noticed another big difference between
these two descriptions. "It was an old white baby shoe" is
pretty low-energy language. Not much going on with
sound or rhythm to catch our attention. But listen to
what's happening up close:

O, that baby boot
that shoe of ivory felt...

Does it sound intense just because it starts with *O*? No, but the *o* sounds an emotional note that is played three more times in just two lines: we go from long *O* to the *oo* in *boot* and *shoe*, then to a modified *o* (closer to *uh*) in *ivory*.

So what?

So sound stirs feeling. When you're hurt -- physically or emotionally -- your first response is not "Whee!" Those long *e's* are too full of energy and excitement. You probably say *oh* or *oo*, or you *moan* because that low open sound expresses pain. And solemnity. Think of Lincoln's opening line of the Gettysburg Address:

Four score and seven years ago our forefathers brought
forth...

In nine words he's given us seven *o's*, five of them the sonorous long o. While you're at it, listen to *sonorous*, too. It means "having or making a rich, deep sound," so the word is an example of itself!

But it's not only the vowel sounds, the a,e,i,o, and u you make by changing the shape of your mouth and vocal chords, that carry feeling. Consonants, which you create by interfering with or stopping the sound with your teeth and tongue, do it, too. For example, in the baby boot lines we have four words which end in *t* -- two *that's*, *boot*, and *felt* -- and their cut-off sound underlines how death has cut people off as well (the dead from their lives, the living and the dead from each other).

There is also tenderness in the *b's* in these lines: *baby boot* (think of nursery words, like babble, bottle, bib, bath) and in the *shhhhh* of *shoe*. So these lines don't carry just one feeling. Part of the power of poetry is that it can express more than one thing at a time. This makes it truer to   experience,   for   who   feels   only   one   thing?

9

Altogether, the repetition and musical movement of sounds (*o* to *oo*, for example) and the rhythm (which I'm coming to) create intense bonds between the words. They hold together, are memorable, not just because of their dictionary meaning but because of their physical effect on us as readers and hearers.

English is what we call a stressed language. We don't distinguish words by pitch, as in some Oriental languages; we don't give signals by clicking noises, as some African languages do. We make distinctions by what part of the word or phrase gets emphasized. For example, how do you tell the difference between "Combine butter and eggs" and "Drive the combine to the field and bale the hay"? How do you know where to go to work? It's the way the word is accented, which part of it your voice stresses.

com*bine* = kitchen
*com*bine = field

Don't panic here. You already know how to use stresses. You talk, and people understand you. Poetry just uses stresses more intensely than we do in everyday speech. For example in

O, that baby boot,
that shoe of ivory felt...

we have three strong stresses in each line. Read it aloud to hear what I mean. And where do they fall? On the *O*, which is both an expression of anguish and a call to pay

10

attention, and on the words which describe the object itself (*baby boot, shoe, ivory, felt*). So the rhythm drums the feeling into us and drives the poem on.

Was I thinking about *o* sounds and stresses when I wrote the first draft of this poem? Not consciously. But to some extent it's natural to choose sound and rhythm that reflect your feeling. And the more poems you read and write, the more natural it becomes. The conscious involvement comes in revising. Wherever I sense a problem, I check the sound and rhythm just as you stop your car and check the tires if the steering wheel wobbles or one part seems to be riding rough. So when you have a draft of your poem, give it a test drive: read it out loud. If anything makes you hesitate, squirm, stumble, or mumble, pull over and have a listen. Like a good mechanic, your ear can sometimes tell you things that your eye misses.

object

This poem began one day when I sat down to write and began studying my hands. (In addition to exercises for writing, I have lots of techniques for Writing Prevention!) It happens that I wear three wedding rings: one from each of my grandmothers and one from my great-grandmother, Ella, whose name I share. I chose to wear these, of course, but until that day I had never really thought about what it meant. Sitting on the tawny rug in my mother-in-law's Hialeah townhouse, it suddenly hit me: I am married to my grandmothers!

Adrienne Rich said, "The moment of change is the only poem," and this realization was such a moment for me. It was as if, hiking a familiar trail, I spotted a cave I'd never noticed before. The writing that followed was like spelunking: I had no idea what I would find, and I often got lost or stuck. The poem wasn't finished for a long time -- months, as I recall. But it started that afternoon with the gleam of Florida sunshine off magic objects: rings.

source

12

RINGS

I married with my grandmother's wedding ring
and wear my great-grandmother's on the other hand,
both too large -- the jeweller cut them down.

Mother and daughter bore seven children,
seven times met death inside out.
Each time they rose and grew larger

like trees, ring on ring, thick with time.
Not all the children lived.
Some were put to bed in iron ground

uncovering the bone-ring of the eye.
Death is its hook -- together they close the gap.
At my grandmother's house we drank from a dipper

long after the backporch pump was gone,
bent and came face to face with water
mouth to metal rim, ring on ring.

13

object

You might look at this title and say, "Hey, wait a minute! A floor is not an object!" And I can see your point. But it is to me because of the way this poem came about. I was leading a workshop using a fabulous book called *The Practice of Poetry*, edited by Robin Behn and Chase Twichell, and I asked the writers to do Rita Dove's exercise, "Your Mother's Kitchen." Before you write about the kitchen (with some specific guidelines), you have to draw it, preferably with a crayon.

We all did this and shared our pictures before heading into words. I was amazed at how different they were! Some folks who I had thought would produce an architectural or a goofy drawing created one that was expressive and detailed. One guy had even drawn the pattern on the linoleum. Seeing that, I realized that the kitchen I had drawn had no floor. I knew why, too. And that's where the poem was.

You try it.

kitchen floor

14

THIS KITCHEN FLOOR

When my mother wanted us
        to go to Europe
on a special deal
        with my brother's senior class
her mother said
        how can you spend the money
with this kitchen floor
        gone crumbly and soft?

and my mother said
        when my children are grown
they'll remember Europe
        they won't remember this floor

but I do   thirty years

its deep blue border
        like the cobalt sky
        one night over Venice
its marbleized swirls
        of indigo and snow
        cerulean and pitch
rich as the rim
        of the baptismal font
in the shadows
        of St. Germain de Près.

BESIDES WRITING ABOUT OBJECTS CLOSE AT HAND, YOU CAN ALSO FOCUS ON OBJECTS FROM YOUR MEMORY OR FROM SOMEONE ELSE'S STORY, AS I DO IN THIS NEXT POEM.

objects of memory

WHEN I WAS GROWING UP, SYRUP CAME IN GLASS BOTTLES, BUT I WAS FASCINATED BY STORIES OF THE BUCKETS OF SYRUP MY MOTHER REMEMBERED FROM HER CHILDHOOD. ONCE THE SYRUP WAS GONE, SHE AND HER FIVE BROTHERS AND SISTERS MADE TOYS OUT OF THE CONTAINER. THE SILVER AND GOLD OF THE SYRUP BUCKET LID MADE IT ELEGANT, AND ITS SHAPE MADE IT AIR-WORTHY, SO THERE WERE LOTS OF POSSIBILITIES FOR PLAY.

BECAUSE HER DADDY WAS A LUMBERMAN, MY MOTHER'S FAMILY MOVED A LOT. THEY HAD TO GO WHEREVER PAPA DAVE COULD GET A BOUNDARY OF TIMBER TO CUT. THE DEPRESSION CAME; MONEY WAS SCARCE, AND MOVING WAS HARD AND TIRESOME. LIKE MANY KIDS, MOTHER SOMETIMES IMAGINED THAT SHE BELONGED IN A MUCH FANCIER WORLD THAN THE MOUNTAINS OF KENTUCKY AND TENNESSEE. THAT'S WHAT THIS POEM IS ABOUT.

16

THE SYRUP BUCKET LID

Round and silver the moon
golden and round the sun
pried off in yet another kitchen,
this time near Billie's Branch.
When the tree's blood was gone
the lid was an ornate tray,
a gleaming disc for a child
to hurl at the sky.
It was a mirror too
for faces not yet set,
for any unknown princess trapped
with a strict family in the sticks.
A strange gift it is,
the sun with its curled lip,
the moon with its face we cannot see
for the dark side of our own.

play

·

In one sense, play is essential to any writing, any art. You have to have the freedom to experiment, turn things upside down, ignore other people's opinions while you're making something. With poetry, you have to get lost (and found) in the language, absorbed in what is happening the way a child forgets everything else while building with Legos or preparing magic food for the elves. Perhaps part of what pushes us to create things is a need for the out-of-time experience such rare concentration brings.

"But wait a minute!" you say. "Writing is WORK." I'll give you that. However, if you go back to the child architect and look at her face, you'll see that it's serious, focused. And, judging from his expression, the chef of leaves and bark could be carrying out a priestly ritual. The truth is, play and work are not opposites. In our deepest work, there is play of mind and spirit, and true play also involves work. We just don't call it that. Isn't playing first base work? Playing the guitar? Playing a part in a play?

We begin to lose our playfulness when we become self-conscious, somewhere around puberty. All of a sudden, we sense we're being judged and so rush to judge ourselves first in hopes of measuring up. This makes creative work especially hard, right at the time when we have so many new things to express!

That's where a journal, or writer's notebook, can help. No one else sees it to judge your writing or your life. "But what do you *put* in a journal?" you may ask. Everything! Dreams, feelings, conversations you don't want to forget, questions, pretend dialogues with different parts of yourself, observations about the world around you, lists of books you've read, movies you've seen, places you want to go. I also use my journal as a scrapbook, gluing or taping in pictures, ticket stubs, pieces of beach grass, leaves, notes, drawings, postcards, sometimes tags from gifts: any little scrap which helps me keep the texture of my life as well as its words. (A spiral-bound journal will accommodate these additions better than a perfect-bound one.) The great thing about the journal is its privacy. I can take risks, I can play and there's nobody there to judge the process.

Play in poetry doesn't mean *no rules*, however. We have to have limits, to make the play meaningful, just as the notebooks' pages can't be free on all sides or there's no notebook. The first poems in this section are haiku, which is a fixed form. That means you have to follow a certain pattern, in this case counting syllables. How can you be free if there are rules? Well, if you remember pretend games, you always set up rules. The Lego builder had a spaceship or other structure in mind which limits the design; the elf-chef has to decide what elves eat and where they live.

Haiku is a Japanese form for which we have developed an English approximation. In three lines, a total of seventeen syllables are balanced, with five syllables in the first line, seven in the second, and five in the third. The goal is to picture a moment of feeling, like a glimpse from a car window. Usually the poem refers to nature or the season and implies some insight about being human. My haiku have titles, though that's not part of the tradition. I just couldn't get everything in seventeen syllables! Or maybe I need to give the reader and the poem more credit and eliminate the titles. See what you think. My references to nature are also less direct than those in most haiku. In "How to Make Bread," I use the four elements -- earth, air, fire, and water -- to describe the magic of the breadmaking process. In "Heart Moving," it's *human* nature I'm talking about, including the nature and structure of the heart.

Some poets use the haiku as a stanza form; that is, each unit of lines set apart by white space follows the haiku pattern. You might want to try this once you get a feel for it.

The other poems in this section set up their own rules but are definitely out to have fun. I hope you will, too!

How to Make Bread

Let air inhabit
earth and water. Lend your weight.
Fire will see it through.

Heart Moving

Heavy, ready, the
walls stripped bare, the opening
and closing of doors.

food play

A FEW YEARS AGO, WRITER AND ARTIST MICHAEL ROSEN ASKED ME TO WRITE A POEM FOR A BOOK CALLED *Food Fight*. SHARE OUR STRENGTH SPONSORED THE PROJECT, SO ALL WORK WAS DONATED, AND THE PROFITS WENT TO FEED THE HUNGRY.

THE GUIDELINES WERE TO CHOOSE A FAVORITE FOOD THAT NO ONE ELSE HAD CHOSEN AND LIMIT THE POEM TO ONE PAGE. DECIDING ON SOUP BEANS WAS EASY. IT'S A STAPLE MEAL WHERE I COME FROM. BUT HOW TO BEGIN? I DIDN'T HAVE A CLUE.

THEN I REMEMBERED THAT, ON PINTO-BEAN NIGHTS WHEN I WAS GROWING UP, MY MOTHER WOULD SAY WE WERE HAVING "THOUSANDS OF THINGS" FOR SUPPER. THAT PLAYFULNESS, PLUS THE SOUND AND RHYTHM OF THE PHRASE, GOT ME STARTED. SOON THE POEM WAS ROCKING THE WAY THE PRESSURE COOKER'S REGULATOR ROCKS WHEN YOU COOK BEANS.

THEN I HIT A SNAG. YOU CAN'T HAVE SOUP-BEANS WITHOUT CORNBREAD, AND ONE FOOD WAS THE LIMIT. I PHONED MICHAEL, PROMISING THAT CORNBREAD WOULDN'T MAKE THE POEM TOO LONG. "OKAY," HE SAID. "BUT NO COLE SLAW."

super soup-beans

FOR A SUPER SOUP-BEAN SUPPER

Take

      hundreds of things
      thousands of things
      look 'em and poke 'em
      soak 'em and cook 'em
      with sowbelly meat
      to make the soup sweet

Get

      a cast-iron skillet
      make batter to fill it

Mix

      corn meal
                 buttermilk
      soda
         egg
            salt
      bacon grease
              baking powder
      can't find
            fault
      with a pone of journey cake
      made just for the sake
      of all those soup beans

'cause strange as it seems
most of my kin grows
on big bowls of pintos
and rich golden rounds
of grown from the ground
corn
        I say   Corn

                        Cornbread!

play *by numbers*

HERE IS ANOTHER FORM BASED ON COUNTING, BUT IN THIS CASE, *you* SUPPLY THE NUMBERS, AND WHAT YOU COUNT IS WORDS, NOT SYLLABLES. WRITE YOUR PHONE NUMBER VERTICALLY ON A SHEET OF PAPER, SKIPPING A LINE BETWEEN THE AREA CODE AND THE THREE-NUMBER PREFIX, AND AGAIN BETWEEN THOSE AND THE FOUR NUMBERS WHICH FOLLOW. THESE ARE YOUR STANZA BREAKS. IF A ZERO IS AMONG YOUR NUMBERS, TREAT IT AS A WILD CARD, ALLOWING YOU TO HAVE AS FEW OR AS MANY WORDS ON THAT LINE AS YOU NEED.

THE FIRST TIME YOU TRY THIS, LET IT BE A SELF-PORTRAIT POEM. AFTER THAT, YOU CHOOSE THE SUBJECT. HERE I COMBINED RESULTS FROM TWO DIFFERENT ATTEMPTS. ONE SECTION IS FROM AN OLD PHONE NUMBER; ONE LEAVES OUT THE AREA CODE.

SELF-PORTRAIT

Tomboy caught
walking Mrs. Haygood's
clothesline, digging to China in the

alley,
running away from home on the traintracks,
painting the doorknobs
red.

*

I would really rather not tell
you
about her. She's wearing that red

dress her
mother got her for her birthday and
she's considering taking up bungee jumping because it's

safer than getting
out of bed. If you ask seven stones why
the creek ran dry, their
voices might remind you of hers.

I HAVE ALWAYS LOVED NEON SIGNS. *SIGN*
ONE DAY WHEN I WAS LOOKING AT A BEAU-
TIFUL BLUE OPEN SIGN, I REALIZED THAT,
IF YOU ADD A SPACE, THE LETTERS SAY O PEN.
FROM THAT, I WENT ON TO SEE THAT OPEN CONSISTS OF
ALMOST THE SAME LETTERS AS POEM. A FEW DAYS LATER
WE WERE ON A FAMILY CAR TRIP. WITH MY HUSBAND DRIVING,
THE BABY ASLEEP IN HIS SEAT, AND OUR OLDER SON LISTENING
TO THE WALKMAN, I BEGAN TO PLAY WITH THE WORDS "O PEN,
OPEN POEM," AND BEFORE TOO MANY MILES I HAD WRITTEN
A DRAFT OF THIS POEM.

play

28

INVOCATION

O pen, open poem.
O paper, pave the way.
O ink, give me inklings
in your dark tongue
what to say.

O letter, let me draw you
out to shape us,
close to hold.
O word, breathe me onward
into mysteries untold.

O sound, sing me deeper
where the soul is so inclined
that if pen open poem,
poem will open
heart and mind.

images

You may look at the word *image* and think, "Oh, no. Poetry talk. I'm not going to understand this." The truth is, you already understand images. You live by them. They are the bulletins your senses bring you about the world. When you get an important bulletin, you keep it, like a snapshot of perception: the smells of the ocean as you walk in the surf, the weight and comfort of a hand on your shoulder, the razzz of the endgame buzzer when you just made the winning point. All of us register these images. Writers turn them into words.

To look at this another way, try for a minute to pretend you are an airport. O'Hare in Chicago would be good since it has so much traffic. Let the in-coming planes be days of your life and the folks who get off each plane be your experiences that day: what you smelled, touched, tasted, heard, and saw. Of course, even a jumbo jet wouldn't begin to hold it all, so imagine that the passengers are only those sensory impressions which made it into your consciousness.

Now if you've ever sat at an airport gate and watched people emerge from the jetway, you know most of them just stream past you, requiring little notice. But a few catch your eye: the Buddhist monk in saffron robes, carrying a laptop; the woman in the long green dress whose tote bag is full of feathers; the man whose business suit doesn't seem to fit with his bright red beard. These few catch your attention, raise questions, stir emotions. Somehow they seem to contain more, to have more possibility than the rest of the crowd. Images are like that. We all experience them. Poets just make them into poems.

33

Let's look at another example. "Rhody," the first poem in this section, is about my great-grandfather's second wife. She was the only grandmother my father knew, and he loved her dearly. But when her husband died, on Valentine's Day of the spring I was born, the anger and resentment his children felt toward her all those years was freed. They threw her out of his house and their lives.

But not before they made her prepare a feast -- during the funeral -- for them to share after they got home. My father told this story with tears in his voice. And it haunted me. One day I felt I had to write about it, so I took the strongest mental picture I had and wrote from there:

RHODY

What I have is an image
an outline in the smokehouse door
arms raised above your thick body
cutting down hams for the funeral dinner.
Everyone gone to the churchhouse
ocean of words washing it
bleak as bone.

They made you stay
though it was your man
heavy in the pine box.
His children forced you
as if in a fairy tale
to prepare them all his goods
to strip yourself of him
and the house of you.

All the weight of them in their worn black suits
the smell in dresses that cut under the arms
laid on you like an iron.

So while they pulled
diamond notes from the hymnal
you worked your old ways --
smokehouse to porch,
pump to castiron stove.
You put your hand
under the plump heat of chickens
gathering one last time
the live stones.

Notice how each of the first four lines brings us
closer to Rhody: image, outline, description, action. The
remainder of the poem explores where that image comes
from and why it matters. Some people call this "unpack-
ing" an image, which fits well with the airport arrival
scene!

Think about strong emotional moments in your
life. You can focus on something recent or an experience
from a long time ago. What images -- sensory images -- do
you have of that time? Which one still hurts or thrills you?
Still scares you or makes you laugh? Write it down just as
you experienced it. Then go back and see if there are sensory
details you left out which could bring the reader closer.
Unpack the image and show us why it matters. If you try
this with four or five different moments, at least one of
them should set you on the road to a poem.

photographic

images

SOMETIMES THE SUBJECT OF YOUR POEM CAN BE A LITERAL IMAGE: A PHOTOGRAPH, A PAINTING, OR A COLLAGE. THE POEM FOLLOWING GOT STARTED WHEN MY FIRST CHILD WAS A PRESCHOOLER, AND I CAME UPON A PICTURE OF MY MOTHER AT ABOUT THE SAME AGE. THEY DIDN'T LOOK ALIKE REALLY, BUT THEY HAD THE SAME LOOK ON THEIR FACES, AND SUDDENLY I WANTED TO BE BOTH THEIR MOTHERS, TO GO BACK AND OFFER THE LITTLE GIRL ON THE PORCH THE KIND OF COMFORT I GAVE TO MY OWN CHILD. THAT'S THE FEELING I TRIED TO CAPTURE IN THE POEM.

LOOKING AT A PHOTOGRAPH
OF MY MOTHER, AGE 3

Little one
in the hand-worked dress
let me lift you
from the porch where you sit
with two brothers and a hound
while your father,
the new baby in his arms,
stands proud
at the gate.
Inside, your mother
beats biscuits, takes
a saucer edge to the meat.

Hard times
line your daddy's hands
with sawdust, hone
your mother's wits
and her tongue.
Seven children
quick as flesh can bear them.
Even deep sleep
cracks
with mouths.

Axe and saw
log hook and level
your daddy shaves hills
for your bread.
Your mother packs up
kettle and quilts
and piano when the sawmill
moves.

Crowded
at the foot
of some mountain
stashed at the head
of some creek
let me lift you.
You can look
like my son
over my shoulder.
I will hold you.
Tell me
what you see.

I GREW UP IN THE COAL-FIELDS OF KENTUCKY AND, LIKE MANY SOUTHERN APPALACHIAN PEOPLE, SAW THE DEVASTATION TO COMMUNITY AND ENVIRONMENT CAUSED BY STRIP MINING. IN THIS PROCESS, THEY REMOVE ALL THE DIRT AND ROCK (PLUS TREES, OTHER VEGETATION, AND WILDLIFE) ABOVE THE COAL SEAM AND THEN DIG OR BLAST THE COAL OUT. DESPITE RECLAMATION EFFORTS (WHICH WEREN'T REQUIRED FOR MANY YEARS), STRIP MINES LEAVE A LEGACY OF UGLY SCARS, BAD WATER, FLOODING, AND LANDSLIDES. "STRIPPED" CAME TO ME ONE DAY WHEN I WAS AT WORK ON THE APPALACHIAN POETRY PROJECT. ON MY DESK I HAD A STACK OF POEM-EVIDENCE OF PEOPLE WHO HAD PROTESTED AND RESISTED THIS DESTRUCTION OF MOUNTAIN LIFE. SOME FOLKS FEEL PROTESTING IS WRONG, THAT YOU SHOULD MIND YOUR OWN BUSINESS. BUT WHEN THE BIGGEST EARTH MOVER IN THE WORLD SHOWS UP AT YOUR GATE, YOU SUDDENLY REALIZE THAT INDUSTRY REGULATION IS YOUR BUSINESS.

i *mountain* ages

STRIPPED

I was humming "Mist on the Mountain"
and shelling peas
I was figuring board feet
I was carting off stones
and quilting lettuce
and thinking about a baby growing ripe inside
I was voting
I was lifting pain out by the roots,
the bread indoors
breathing beneath a thin towel,
when a D-10 dozer came
and rolled me off the front porch.

images

of white gloves

Years before his own death, my father was a pallbearer at a neighbor's funeral. I had seen him perform this task before, but somehow that day was different. As soon as I saw his hands in the white gloves, I knew for the first time that my father would die someday, too. Of course, we know we're all going to die, but that's not the same as feeling the truth of that fact about someone you love, someone central to your life. That's where this poem came from.

PALLBEARERS

Strong hands in white gloves
cloth smooth as flour,
silent men come down the aisle
at the end of tremulous song.
White hands from black coat sleeves
grasp brass handles
White hands beneath the load
help shoulder grief.

You carried many a
neighbor and friend
from the churchhouse
to Resthaven.
Daddy, when you took
the white hand of death
was there singing
on the other side?

41

As you probably figured out, poems usually happen through lots of images, not just one. Images work together to build or deepen an effect, to help us see and feel in many directions at the same time. Someone once defined the poet as a person who can't stand to say just one thing at a time, and the interaction of images helps create that multi-dimensional effect.

Going back to "Rhody," the poem pulls us close to her through a series of images, but it begins with one. "Looking at a Photograph...." fills in the scene of the photograph with images in the first stanza, gives background information through images in the second stanza, and then, again through images, pulls the past and the present together in the final stanza. "Stripped" is primarily a list of images leading up to the wallop of the last one, and "Pallbearers" tunnels into the image of the white-gloved hand until it becomes, at the end, the hand of Death itself.

Before leaving this talk of images, I need to touch down at the airport one more time. When I asked you to imagine that you were an airport, I was putting you at the center of a type of imagery called *metaphor*. I didn't say "Pretend you're *like* an airport" -- that's a less radical form of comparison called a *simile* -- I asked for very close identification, transfer of some of the airport's qualities to you. If simile is like holding hands, metaphor is kissing. *Metaphor* is, in fact, the Greek word for transfer, and a friend of mine once saw, from her hotel window in Athens, a semi-truck roll by with the company name METAPHOR painted in huge letters on the side. You may have seen the tee-shirt which says "METAPHORS be with you!" They always will be, whether we write poems or not, because they are a basic way we have to understand and connect with the world.

shape

How can you tell that a piece of writing means to be a poem without even reading it? By its shape, right? By all that white space around it. Poets use space the way sculptors do: carving a shape on the page to give their words plenty of room and attention. But the shape of the poem isn't only about how it looks; it's about how to read it. The line breaks and stanza breaks give the voice directions for reading just as a page of music tells the musician what and how to play.

When you're writing a poem, and you choose to break a line at a certain point, you are affecting not only the visual shape but the shape of sound the poem makes. You're creating a pause or stop, and you're adding emphasis to the end-word of that line and the beginning word of the next. You emphasize not only their meaning but their sound, so you are directing the music of the poem, too. (If you're writing in rhyme, the emphasis on the end word is obvious, but it's there without rhyme as well.) The way shape works will make more sense if we look at a specific poem.

CHOICE

Recollect now
how it was with her
Winter
and two kids

> no work, no wood,
> no man
> and not a soul of us caring
> that she'd boiled the marrow
> out of what bones she had,
> then fed the bed to the fire
> and her kids still
> blue-cold and whimpering.
> Ma'll get you warm, she said,
> and the whole house went.

Because the first line breaks after "now," we experience "Recollect now" as a call to stop and think. We pause for a split second at the end of the line, and it's just enough time to let those two words bond and ring out together. Likewise, "how it was with her" is given more substance by being on a line by itself than it would have if the first two lines were one. By breaking them, the poem gives equal weight to the recollecting reader and to "how it was with" the woman, to us and to her. And that's what the poem is about.

"Winter," the next line, is only one word, so that the season and its harsh reality can soak in. It is followed by three lines which tell us the hard facts of this individual's life:

> Winter
> and two kids
> no work, no wood
> no man

What she has -- the cold and the kids -- is tallied up with what she doesn't have. And her desperate situation is emphasized by "Winter" and "no man" being the shortest lines in the poem, each only two syllables. She is cornered. Even so, tragedy will not be inevitable if someone in the community intervenes. But the speaker tells us, in the first of a series of longer, looser lines, that no one comes to this family's rescue:

> and not a soul of us caring
> that she's boiled the marrow
> out of what bones she had
> split table and chairs
> then fed the bed to the fire

Even this extreme action is not enough, as the next lines reveal:

> and her kids still
> blue-cold and whimpering

See how the first line is suddenly short, as if the words contracted because of the cold? And see how "still" works two ways when it comes at the end of the line? Its first meaning is that the kids' condition hasn't changed, but because of where it comes, we also see their stillness, feel them huddled together, too hungry and cold to move. As the next line lengthens out, we hear them appealing to their mother for help. By this point in the poem, we know the wall this woman is up against, but we have no idea what action she will take.

The lines which convey that action continue the plain language typical of the whole poem -- it has only eight words with more than one syllable. But the ordinary words only intensify its horror:

> **Ma'll get you warm, she said,**
> **and the whole house went.**

"Choice" uses space in a fairly standard manner; its line breaks guide the voice but don't suggest a picture or make great leaps in space or time. Some poems do. Sometimes a poem works best if you let its visual shape reflect its content more graphically, as in the pieces which follow. I didn't set out to write a picture. I just tried that when I wasn't getting anywhere in the regular mode.

Be aware that you are always choosing a shape for your poem: long lines or short lines, even margins or ragged, the number and length of stanzas. At the same time, remember that you always have the option of a more radical shape. Give it a try sometime when you're writing about a particularly visual image or when you are stuck.

I get stuck sometimes, too, and it's not a good feeling. It's as if the words just dry up. But I've developed some strategies for dealing with the situation. If experimenting with shape doesn't work, I might pick the line that interests me most and do some free-writing from there. Or I might turn the paper over, write at the top "What I'm Not Saying Is," and see what pops out. Sometimes there really is a block; something is in the way, and I have to look at it. I may still decide not to use it in the poem, but at least I know what it is!

The only way to tell if a more graphic shape will help your poem is to play with it. Just be sure you keep all your drafts, so you can go back to an earlier version if you feel the experiment isn't working. The writing time won't be lost either. Like a tightrope walker on the line, you'll be learning about space, that thrilling and perilous place where poems live.

shape

poems with a backbone

THIS POEM BEGAN WHEN MY SECOND BABY GOT HIS FIRST BRUISE. THAT MAY NOT STRIKE YOU AS SOMETHING TO WRITE ABOUT, BUT JUST CONSIDER IT A MINUTE. HERE'S A CREATURE WHOSE SKIN IS UNMARKED. HE'S NEVER BEEN SCRATCHED, PINCHED, WOUNDED. AS A PARENT, YOU WANT IT TO BE THAT WAY ALWAYS, BUT YOU KNOW IT WON'T. AND WHEN THE FIRST INJURY COMES, HOWEVER SLIGHT IT IS, YOU KNOW THE DOOR IS OPEN FOR ALL THE SUFFERING BODIES CAN ENDURE. LIKE "WHERE I'M FROM," "O" STARTED AS A LIST. IT WAS MUCH LONGER THAN THE POEM YOU SEE HERE, AND THE ITEMS WERE NOT IN THIS ORDER. MOST IMPORTANT FOR THE POEM'S CREATION, I ONLY USED A FEW O'S AT FIRST, AND THEY WERE AT THE BEGINNING OF LINES, NOT AT THE CENTER. THEN, AS I READ THE DRAFTS OUT LOUD, I REALIZED THAT "O" WAS A CRY, THE BACKBONE OF THE POEM. THUS, THIS SHAPE.

O

blue bumps
tightening the forehead
O
pump knots
stretching the scalp
O
beaded knees
grated on a steel mat
O
shiny palms
burned on a floor
O
wrenched elbows
throwing to home plate
O
purple fingers
slammed in doors
O
oozing toes
stung in the ocean
O
blistered shoulders
weeping in the field
O
peeled arm
slid down a hickory

O
slit belly
fallen on a knife
O
red scarf
right where the eye was
O
stopped heart
wide mouth
O

hand *shape*

ONCE I TOLD MY CREATIVE WRITING CLASS: "LOOK AT YOUR HAND. WRITE WHAT YOU SEE AND REMEMBER." I DID IT, TOO. WHAT I CAME UP WITH WAS A LIST OF IMAGES, BUT I COULDN'T FIGURE OUT A WAY TO CONNECT THEM. A YEAR LATER, I WAS PAGING THROUGH OLD JOURNALS AND THAT EXERCISE LEAPED OUT AT ME. WHAT I SAW THAT I HAD MISSED ON THE DAY OF WRITING WAS THE FORCE OF THE LINE "I HOLD IT UP." IT COULD BE REPEATED WITH DIFFERENT MEANING AT DIFFERENT POINTS IN THE POEM TO BRING IT TOGETHER. I BEGAN TO WORK ON THIS, MOVING IMAGES AROUND, TAKING SOME OUT, REWORDING OTHERS. STILL, IT DIDN'T QUITE COME ALIVE. THEN I THOUGHT ABOUT THE HAND AGAIN. MAYBE THE POEM COULD ACTUALLY TAKE THAT SHAPE! MAYBE THAT'S WHAT IT WANTED. NOW I WAS REALLY HAVING FUN: DRAWING A LITTLE HANDSHAPE, CUTTING UP THE WORDS AND TRYING TO FIT THEM INTO IT. AT ONE POINT, THE WORDS ALL STUCK TO MY FINGERS, AND I REALIZED THE PICTURE I WAS TRYING TO CREATE HAD BECOME REAL: A HAND OF WORDS. LAUGHING, I HELD IT UP.

CALL ON ME

I hold it up

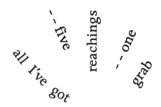

this scarecrow mitt
this wave of a drowning
this truce

I hold it up
like my mother used to do
when she slipped my hand
through ruffled sleeves
till she smoothed the cloth
down over my self
and I reached to be
picked up

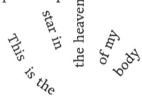

this handle
that lets
everything go

I hold it up

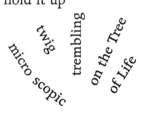

53

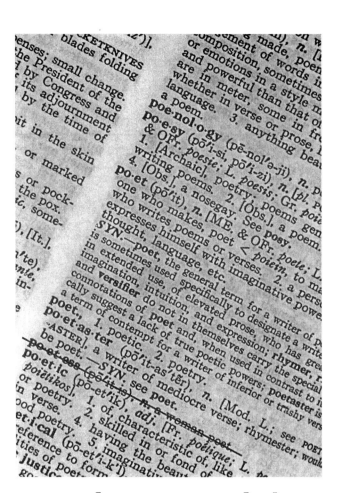

other people's
words

There is a kind of poem — the found poem — which you don't even have to write! You create it by looking for more significance in the language around you than the speaker or writer intended and arranging the found words on the page so that readers will see it, too. You may discover your material anywhere: in signs, memos, conversations, letters and diaries, advertisements, whatever gets your attention. For example, last summer when I was driving in my native territory, the mountains of Kentucky, I saw this handmade sign tacked up at a turnoff:

NIGHTCRAWLERS — THIRD HOUSE ON THE LEFT

Now I know the writer was just trying to sell bait to passing fishermen. That's one level of the message. But on another level, it can lead a reader to imagine taking that little road and pulling up at a house full of slithery figures whose red eyes vibrate at every window. I haven't used this in a poem yet, but you can bet I put it in my journal. Who knows what I will find to go with it?

The only rules for the found poem are that you must credit your source(s) and that you don't use material which already has literary intentions. After all, to find a poem in a novel is not that much of a transformation. To find one in talk overheard in a fast-food place is.

The other restrictions are up to you. Will you leave things out? Rearrange them? Add a few of your own words? Use more than one source?

The key is to pay attention and develop the habit

57

of seeing the words around you in new ways. What meaning do they carry that the speaker or writer was unaware of? How can you craft them so that the reader sees or hears what you did?

Like more conventional poems, the found poem is intended to convey your particular vision; in this case, your vision of words at work in the world. So, after sampling the found poems here, set out in search for one of your own. Besides sources I've already mentioned, you might try looking in newspaper headlines and personal ads or making a list of your favorite answering machine messages and song titles. Perhaps you could explore a theme by combining words from different sources. Experiment. There are possibilities for poetry all around you, so be watchful, carry a notebook, and don't be afraid to play with what you find!

other people's words

ONE DAY WHEN MY YOUNGER SON WAS IN THIRD GRADE, HE BROUGHT HOME A MEMO FROM HIS TEACHER. HANDWRITTEN, IT ASKED EVERYBODY TO LOOK AT HOME FOR SOMETHING WHICH HAD DISAPPEARED FROM THE CLASSROOM. AS SOON AS I CAME TO "THE HEART IS MISSING," I KNEW THIS WASN'T JUST A MEMO; IT HAD THE MAKINGS OF A POEM. TO SHAPE THE MATERIAL IN THAT DIRECTION, ALL I DID WAS LEAVE OUT A FEW WORDS, MOVE "DEAR PARENTS" AWAY FROM THE BEGINNING, REPEAT "PLEASE," AND BREAK THE LINES WHERE MY VOICE NATURALLY PAUSED. EXCITED, I TYPED IT UP, ONLY TO BE DISAPPOINTED. IT DIDN'T HAVE THE SAME EFFECT WITHOUT THE TEACHER'S URGENT HANDWRITING. SO I XEROXED THE MEMO, THEN CUT AND PASTED IT TO FORM WHAT YOU SEE BELOW. (I ALSO SHOWED IT TO THE TEACHER AND GOT HER PERMISSION TO PUBLISH IT.)

MARILYNN'S MONTESSORI MEMO
-- *a found poem*

In connection with the study
of the human body
I borrowed a plastic model
with removable parts
Unfortunately
I left it out to view
and the heart is missing.

It is about the size
of a dried date
shaped and painted
to look like a heart.
Dear Parents,
If you find it at home
PLEASE PLEASE
return it.

other people's words

conversations

THE SUMMER MY OLDER SON WAS FOUR, HE ASKED ME AN AMAZING SET OF QUESTIONS. THEY DIDN'T COME ALL IN ONE CONVERSATION, AS I HAVE THEM HERE, BUT WERE SPREAD OUT OVER SEVERAL DAYS. UNTIL THE FINAL QUESTION, I DIDN'T REALIZE THAT THEY FIT TOGETHER, AND THAT HE HAD BEEN WORKING HIS WAY TO THE LAST ONE ALL ALONG. I WAS STUNNED, AND SO I MADE THE POEM TO TRY TO SHARE THE EXPERIENCE AND PASS THAT FEELING ON.

THE ORDER OF THE QUESTIONS IS THE ONE IN WHICH HE ASKED THEM, BUT THERE WAS A LOT MORE TALK BETWEEN THEM WHICH I LEFT OUT. THE PROCESS IS SORT OF LIKE WEEDING A FLOWERBED. YOU PULL OUT WHATEVER DISTRACTS FROM THE WHOLE EFFECT YOU WANT.

CATECHISMS

-- poem found in conversations
with a four-year-old

What's the oldest thing that's living?
>Trees probably -- California redwoods.

I mean that moves around.
>A tortoise I guess.

No, I mean that moves around and talks:
the oldest thing.
>Some person somewhere.

Are your bones going to come through?
>What?

When your sunburn peels, are your bones
going to poke through?
>No, no, there's new skin under there.
>It's tough.

Will they ever?
>Not unless I get a bad break.

Don't do that.
>No.

They'd have to put you in the hard stuff.
>What?

The white bone stuff. They'd have to put it
all over.
>That's called a cast.

Do they sew bones?
>No, bones can grow back together.

Who will die first?

other people's words

Once when I was chaperoning my son's Cub Scout hike, I got to talking with two other chaperones: Bill, a building contractor and Jim, a former fighter pilot. Because a cache of letters had been found in the wall of a house Bill was remodeling, we began discussing the fascination of old letters and diaries. Jim said he had several Civil War diaries at home if I'd like to look at them. Would I!

Over the next few weeks, I read them all -- crying, laughing, and marvelling at the lost life that leapt from their pages. Before I gave them back, I realized that some entries made poems all by themselves. Not a word moved, left out, or added. All I needed to do was create line breaks for breath and dramatic effect. Unfortunately, I couldn't photocopy Mr. Roberts' handwriting because it's mostly in faded pencil and because the diaries -- which are only 4" x 2" -- are too fragile to take the handling and the copier light. I decided that the next-best thing would be to write the poems out myself, to preserve the intimate feeling of reading someone's diary.

62

POEMS FOUND IN THE DIARIES OF JAMES H. ROBERTS OF LONDON, OHIO

Thursday April 30, 1863

This is a day
set aside by the President
for fasting and prayer
in consideration
of our great troubles.

I feel as though all the prayers
that can be made in the U.S.
will not affect God's purposes
but they may have a salutary effect
on utterers and hearers.

Thursday May 19, 1864

Clear warm and pleasant
Sent $2.25 to R.T. Trall for books.
My wife presented me
with a large boy weighing 11 pounds
today at 7 o'c in the evening
Bot Soap Grease + Eggs 35¢

Tuesday July 5, 1864

D. B. Warner
has lost an arm in battle –
Jesse Dunigan
was wounded in the leg.
His father got a dispatch today
that he was _dead_ =
Cursed be the men
who started this war –
Got a letter from P.L.R. today
– wants two shirts – is well –
Says C.C. Roberts
is wounded in thigh
a flesh wound –

Monday June 6, 1864

Nothing very startling.
Grant is before Richmond
Sherman is "pushing on to Atlanta."

other people's words

BECAUSE I SPEND SO MUCH TIME STANDING IN LINE AT THE GROCERY STORE, I DECIDED TO TAKE UP WRITING THERE. I KNEW I WOULDN'T HAVE THE KIND OF CONCENTRATION TO WRITE OR REVISE NEW WORK, SO I CHOSE TO WRITE DOWN STUFF THAT WAS GOING ON AROUND ME: BITS OF CONVERSATION, SCENES IN THE CHECKOUT LANE, WORDS BLARING FROM MAGAZINES AND TABLOIDS ON THE RACK OPPOSITE THE GUM AND CANDY. "SOMEDAY I'LL DO SOMETHING WITH THIS," I THOUGHT. MEANWHILE, IT KEPT ME FROM BEING BORED.

AT THE SAME TIME, I WAS WRITING (IN A LARGER NOTE-BOOK) QUOTATIONS FROM FRIENDS IN MY WRITERS' GROUP. WE MEET ONCE A MONTH, BRINGING FOOD FOR LUNCH, AND SPEND MOST OF THE DAY READING AND TALKING ABOUT EACH OTHERS' WORK. I WASN'T PLANNING TO DO ANYTHING WITH THESE WORDS; THEY WERE JUST TOO WONDERFUL TO LET GO. CHRISTMAS ROLLED AROUND, AND I WANTED TO MAKE A GIFT FOR THE GROUP. SINCE WE'RE ALWAYS TALKING ABOUT HOW HARD IT IS TO WRITE AND ALSO TAKE CARE OF THE OTHER NECESSITIES OF LIFE -- HOME, FAMILY, JOBS, SELF -- I THOUGHT THAT MAKING A POEM BY INTERCUT-TING QUOTATIONS FROM BOTH SOURCES WOULD EMPHASIZE THE STRUGGLE AND BE FUN BESIDES. HERE IS THE RESULT:

check-out conversation

GAZING INWARD AND CHECKING OUT

-- poem found in conversations at my writers' group
and in the spectacle of the check-out line at the grocery

I say to myself I'm having this crazy life
because I'm supposed to write about it.

*Kevin, the checker, can't get his pen to work. Shakes it, licks
it. I offer mine.*

I've been trying for two weeks
to think of another word for *betrayed*.

Gee, thanks, Doris.

You do have to carve out
a smooth place in your life
to write stuff that is not smooth.

*Shape Up with Foods
That Boost Your Moods*

I kind of feel like I'm writing
one word at a time
into a very dark place.

*A woman in a giraffe-patterned coat gives a little shimmy in
front of the scanner and says, "O-oo-oo, I'm going to make
cupcakes tonight!"*

How is the life not the work?

Unleashing the Sex Goddess in Every Woman

> He's not anybody I'd pick out of a crowd
> -- or even out of a small group.

Your Child's Brain

> He had eleven sandwiches in his room!

Are You Tired of Fatigue?

> I hope to get back to work
> as soon as I get the mop off the porch.

A woman comes in and says, "I'm pushing my groceries to the car? Halfway across the parking lot a phone in the cart rings! It's the owner who doesn't know where he left it."

> If your writing makes you afraid,
> that's a good sign.

Get the Body You Want

> You knew when you got near that fire
> it didn't matter what your mother said.

This checker wears purple nails, a flannel shirt, gold rings on every finger. She flirts with the bagger as she scans a magazine full of FAT-BURNING RECIPES. "When do you get off?" he asks, tossing his dreadlocks. "I'm not going to tell you that," she answers.

That's one of the things
my husband brought to our marriage.
I guess this should have been a warning.

Twins are talking to each other, one in Daddy's cart, one in Mama's. The twin in my lane plays Look-inside-Daddy's-jacket.

Of course I've had lots of therapy, like everybody
else but now it's *fun.*

Sign over closed Express Lane says: All Lanes Open.

My sons says, "I'm not black. I'm brown.
And nobody pays attention to that anymore,
Mom." Yet he gets beaten up on the bus.

Ten New Ways to Please Your Man

It can take a long time to figure out how slow
things are.

Change Your Life -- Today!

I've had nothing but turmoil
since I tried to seek inner peace.

"GAZING INWARD..." IS DIFFERENT FROM THE OTHER FOUND
POEMS HERE SINCE, IN ADDITION TO OVERHEARD TALK AND PRINTED
WORDS, I ALSO USE MY OWN WORDS TO DESCRIBE A FEW SCENES. BUT,
AS I SAID, WITH FOUND POEMS YOU CAN MAKE UP YOUR OWN RULES. I
HOPE YOU DO. GOOD LUCK.

voices

You probably don't realize it, but you have lots of voices stored in your memory. Many are of the people who nurtured you -- parents, grandparents, aunts, uncles. Others are from the larger circle of neighborhood and community -- friends, teachers, a doctor perhaps, people from where you worship. Then there are the voices of your best friends and the first person you had a crush on, plus voices from the news, movies, T.V.

All your life you've listened and recorded the different ways people talk and what they talk about. Some of this has a lot of emotional weight, and you can explore that weight, maybe lift it for a while, by writing in another person's voice.

But how can you retrieve a voice? Like any other weight-lifting it takes practice. Here's one way to get started.

Put away all distractions, get quiet, and consider which voice you are most likely to remember or are most drawn to write from. When you have chosen, write down three things you have heard that person say. Don't panic. These don't have to be whole sentences, much less speeches. Phrases are okay. For example, what does the person say in greeting? What does s/he call you? Does s/he have a favorite expression? Listen for the voice in your memory.

When you've done that, you can leave the actual voice for awhile and answer some questions. Again, this doesn't have to be in sentences; just write enough so that you know what you mean. If you don't know an answer, take what you *do* know of the person and imagine an answer from that. If this happens, and the voice in your poem becomes more of an invention than a real person, that's okay, too. You've just taken a step toward creating a character!

1) What place, indoors or outdoors, is really important to this person?

2) Name a dream he or she has. (It could be a nighttime dream or a dream in the sense of a longing or a goal.)

3) Does this person have a favorite object -- piece of jewelry, something kept in the bedroom, on the desk or windowsill, in the car? What is it?

4) What is this person's biggest fear? (It may be a literal fear, like that of snakes, or an abstract one, like the fear of being exposed as a fraud.)

5) What is his or her favorite meal? Where would s/he prefer to eat it?

6) What makes this person really mad?

7) What is his or her secret?

There could be many more questions on this list -- you may think of some to add -- but seven is a good, magical number, so I'll stop here.

The next step is to look back over your answers and pick one which interests you most, which has the most energy for you. Then comes the leap.

Imagine that you are the person you have chosen (you may even want to picture what clothes you have on) and let him or her tell about the subject you selected: place, dream, object, fear, meal, anger, or secret. Remember, it's not *you* telling what you think your person thinks or feels. It's him or her talking. Speaking in first person. Saying *I*. You just get out of the way.

You may protest, "But, I don't know how to do that!" The truth is, I don't know how either; I just know that sometimes I try it, and it works. Remember when you were a kid and you played Pretend? You might do it with dolls or action figures, with friends, or just on your own. Writers go on pretending. We just use language instead of acting things out. You can do it. You just have to loosen up.

An important element of that process is suspending judgment of your first draft. Don't worry if it's in paragraphs instead of poetic lines, or if the person switches subjects, or the voice seems to change. Just keep going until you've got all he or she has to say, then read it aloud to see how the voice sounds. This may help you decide what to add or leave out, where the lines should break, etc. When you've got it in poem-shape, read it to a small group and listen to their poems as well. Everybody benefits from questions, suggestions, and examples of how other people work. After this session, you can revise further.

Sometimes the person you choose to listen to doesn't work out. Maybe she won't talk or doesn't have much that is interesting to say. Don't be discouraged. It happens to me a lot. Just try again with another speaker and be patient with yourself while you're getting the hang of it. I've done this exercise for years, and I never know how it will work out. It's a little like fishing: some days you catch fish; other days you just enjoy being near the water. Happy listening!

voices

"WARNING" CAME RIGHT OUT OF THE EXERCISE I HAVE GIVEN YOU. I WAS DOING IT WITH A CLASS, AND THE PERSON WHOSE VOICE I LISTENED FOR WAS MY FATHER'S. AS YOU CAN TELL, THIS IS ABOUT WHAT MADE HIM MAD.

WARNING

I don't understand why
a person cannot find
a hammer in this house.
I have a tool box.
I have a tool drawer.
You take something,
you should put it back.

In a heartbeat, my daddy
could lay his hand
on any one of a hundred tools.
It wouldn't be rusty
or have a handle loose either.
There wouldn't be putty stuck to it
or the blade bent or the hinge missing.

I am not a demanding man.
I am not fastidious about any
of the rest of my things.
If you took my best shirt and swabbed the car with it
I could let that go.
You could drive the car itself
to Kingdom Come and back,
put a dent in it while you're at it,
I don't care.
But when I need my Fuller 215
7/16 socket wrench
with the translucent yellow handle
and the red head --
I'm telling you
next time I reach for that tool
it better be there.

voices

storytellers'

I come from a family and a part of the country where stories, and those who can bring them alive in the telling, are highly valued. One of our best storytellers when I was growing up was my grandmother's first cousin, Ella (In the photo she is the one on the right). Her back door was not fifty feet from ours, and she often came over, usually bearing food. If it was summer, she might bring fried apples; if it was Christmas, she'd come carrying peanut butter roll or stack cake. Whatever the season, she brought stories.

When I first tried to write in her voice, I hid a tape recorder on the piano and asked her to tell the one about driving to Texas on retreads. My plan was to transcribe the recording and have a poem. Well, I transcribed it all right, but the result didn't have the liveliness, the sparkle of her telling. I realized then that writers can't copy a voice (or a situation from life); we have to create an illusion of it, in language that has more focus, meaning, and verbal drive than the original, yet still sounds natural. Somehow I had to get the essence of Ella into the poem, had to let her enchant the reader as she always enchanted me.

The retreads poem is in the "Stories" section. This one is from a story she told only to my mother about the time she made a break from her life in our small mountain town.

78

COUSIN ELLA GOES TO TOWN

Now you have to promise
you won't breathe a word of this.
It was after Brian died.
You know I got me a little insurance money
and I said to myself, Eller,
what kind of life have you had
and what are you likely to get
and you know the answer to that.
Not much.

Seemed like all I'd ever done
was dump pennies from a jar.
Brian left me just enough
to stay on in this house,
sewing and tending other people's kids
fading out like an old TV
So I took a hard look.
And do you know what I did?

I went to Louisville.
Yes, sir, I got on the Greyhound bus
rode right there
and took a taxi to the Galt House
and for four days
I had me a room
and I pretended
to be somebody else.

Lord, children, I ate the best food
went to dress stores and picture shows
I even called my name different.
And do you know
I got so high and mighty
with my new hairdo --
I had the yellow scared out of this wad
got me a city style --
that on the third night
right before the IceCapades
I was trying on this hat
and I saw my face all gaudy in that mirror
and my freckled hands
with peach polish on each nail
and I took to crying
for all the world like Brian had died again.

I grabbed a washrag
and scrubbed my face.
I snatched them bobby pins out of my hair
and brushed it till my scalp
stung like fire.
And, honey, I got out of there.

By the time the bus let me off
I was plumb out of tears.
I just marched in
put my pocketbook down --
I'd left everything but a new raincoat
at the hotel --
I rolled down my stockings
heated up some soup
sat in my chair

and read the Sunday School lesson.
Next morning I tried
to wear that coat to church
but you know it never fit me right
at all.

from the heart

voices

IN AUGUST, 1981, I WAS SITTING IN ON SHIRLEY
WILLIAMS' NONFICTION CLASS AT THE APPALACHIAN
WRITERS WORKSHOP, AND SHE TOLD THIS STORY: ONE
SUNDAY WHEN SHE WAS A KID, SHE WAS WALKING HOME
FROM CHURCH, AND HER GRANDDADDY, WHO WAS NOT A
CHURCHGOER, CALLED TO HER FROM HIS WORK IN THE GARDEN,
"SHIRLEY, WHAT ARE YOU SO HAPPY ABOUT?"

"WELL, GRANDDADDY," SHE REPLIED, "VIRGIL
COLLETT GAVE HIS HEART TO THE LORD THIS MORNING."
HER GRANDDADDY'S REPLY BECAME THE INSPIRATION, AND THE EPI-
GRAPH, FOR THIS POEM.

SALVATION

What does the Lord want with Virgil's heart?
And what is Virgil going to do without one?

O Lord, spare him the Call.
You're looking for bass
in a pond stocked with catfish.
Pass him by.
You got our best.
You took Mammy and the truck and the second hay.
What do You want with Virgil's heart?

Virgil, he comes in of a night
so wore out he can hardly chew
blacked with dust that don't come off at the bathhouse.
He washes again
eats onions and beans with the rest of us
then gives the least one a shoulder ride to bed
slow and singing
> *Down in some lone valley*
> *in some lonesome place*
> *where the wild birds do whistle...*[*]

After that, he sags like a full feed sack
on a couch alongside the TV
and watches whatever news Your waves are giving.
His soul sifts out
like feed from a slit in that sack
and he's gone
wore out and give out and plumb used up, Lord.
What do you want with his heart?

* I always sing that little piece of "Pretty Saro" when I come to it in "Salvation." If music is important to you, you may want to try weaving bits of songs in your poems, too.

stories

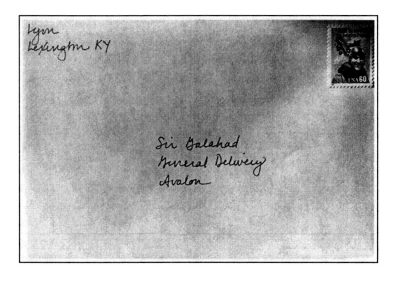

Lyon
Lexington KY

Sir Galahad
General Delivery
Avalon

USA 60

One of my favorite definitions of a human is "the creature without feathers who tells stories." I like it because it shows how basic stories are, how necessary to us. "But stories," you might say, "are just entertainment." Well, even if that were true, entertainment is pretty important, too. Literally, the word means "to hold between," and stories do that. They hold us between our own lives and someone eise's, so that we are relieved of our singularity for a moment and can get a different perspective. Stories let us experience the possibilities of Life -- cowardice, heroism, greed, faithfulness -- and glimpse the shape of our own lives. So stories are precious possessions.

"That's fine," you may say, "but I don't have any stories, except what I get off TV." You do, though. You just haven't felt the need to pay attention to them. Do you live in a family? That's a story collection in itself: how your parents got together (whether they're still together or not), how they wound up living where they do, how they chose (or got pushed into) the work they do, what happened the day you were born. Have you ever moved? There's a story. Been lost? Gone on a trip? Done something really dumb? All of these experiences contain the seeds of story. And, if you listen to your conversation with friends, you'll find you tell bits of stories all the time: why I was late to practice, what happened Friday night, how the French teacher got locked in the supply closet.

Okay, but if you have a story, why not write it out in prose? Why bother with line breaks and all the paraphernalia of poetry? For starters, a poem is a very compact container for a story, as different from prose as a wallet on a string is from a suitcase on wheels. By the same token, because it's relatively short and makes maximum use of sound and rhythm, the narrative poem will have a different kind of concentration and intensity than the short story.

There are disadvantages, too, of course. You have to leave a lot of things out. But what's left in can be thrilling.

So where do you start? One way is to begin with a list of incidents you could write about. Put this in your journal so you can come back to it. Remember, the incidents could have happened to somebody besides you. Then pick one that you have an emotional connection to and write it out in whatever way it comes to you: a list, a paragraph, a scene. When you've finished, look it over. Where could you add details that will wake up the reader's senses? Is there an image that stands out? Is there a person other than you who could tell this story? (See "Voices.") What would happen if you began by telling the end and then told the events leading up to it?

These questions, and others you may come up with, will give you different ways to approach the poem. When you've reflected on them, look at the words you've written so far and listen in your head for a place to start. When something comes to you, don't second-guess it! Write it down and then take off in whatever direction it calls you. Follow that lead through the story, breaking lines where the voice pauses. When you come to the end, read it over and see what you've got. You may love it or may feel it's not on the right path. You may sort of like it but not know what to do next. In that case, try it out on friends. Listen to their questions and comments. Check the sound. But don't be discouraged if the first go-round doesn't seem right. You haven't lost anything: the story is still there. Go back and try another approach. You'll be learning all the way.

You see, writing is like any other discipline -- like dancing, say, or playing a sport. To be good, you have to spend a lot of time practicing, learning the moves, gaining strength and agility. You don't expect to put on leotards or pick up a basketball one day and be in a recital or a tournament the next. Be patient. If you're really trying, nothing is wasted. Someday, when the crowd's shouting, and you're at the free-throw line, you'll be glad you shot a million baskets. And you'll forget all those blisters on your toes when the house lights go down, and it's time to dance *Swan Lake*.

stories

My grandmother told me this story, long after my grandfather had died. It gave me a glimpse of him I'd never had before: the youngest kid, teased by the older ones but determined to track down the mysteries of life.

mystery

PAPAW

They told him, the youngest,
that babies came from coal mines
so when the Wilders up the creek had their last
he went to see.
He didn't take the mine road
but chose the path by the tipple.
Some journeys shouldn't be easy even in the dark.

At daybreak
when he came in the yard
Dillard and Minnie were smiling.
It ain't true, he said,
coal dust streaking his face.
I been there and there ain't no tracks.

legendary stories

"WHAT BEGAN AT THE POST OFFICE" IS THE OLD-
EST POEM IN THIS COLLECTION, AND I REALLY DON'T KNOW
WHERE IT CAME FROM. WHEN I WROTE IT IN 1975, I WAS
FAMILIAR WITH THE STORIES OF KING ARTHUR, AND KNEW
THAT SIR GALAHAD, SON OF LANCELOT AND ALAIN, WAS
THE ONE TO FIND THE HOLY GRAIL. BUT I HADN'T BEEN
READING OR THINKING ABOUT THESE THINGS. NOR DID I
HAVE CHILDREN THEN, AS THE SPEAKER IN THE POEM DOES.
I JUST GOT UP ONE MORNING, TOOK COFFEE TO MY DESK,
LISTENED FOR A PLACE TO BEGIN, AND THE FIRST TWO LINES CAME TO
ME. I SET OUT TO FOLLOW THEM WITH NO IDEA OF WHERE THE POEM
WAS GOING.

WHAT BEGAN AT THE POST OFFICE

When I saw Sir Galahad, I said, "Peace be with you."
He smiled, but was so shaken he dropped his stamps.
I asked if he'd like to come visit and share his stories;
he only stared at the beatup Timex watch.
"I've a daughter, " I ventured, "just thirteen this summer
and a son who's read all the King Arthur tales.
They'd love to meet you." At this his eyes grew sadder.
"All right," he murmured, and shouldered a drawstring bag.

Soon he sat stockstill by the dining-room window
looking at the dogwood tree and the weedy lawn.

"The kids'll be home from school any minute, " I promised,
setting down cheese and crackers and wine and milk.
Galahad's eyes lit up like next year's pennies;
he lifted the wine bottle off its wooden tray,
he drank straight down halfway past the label
then leaned forward, the bottle on his knee.
"O far away," he said to the Persian carpet,
"deep in the wells of the world we laid him down,
there where swans like clouds would glide above him
and reeds and cattails keep a gentle edge.
I don't believe he was taken to that city.
No, in the water's wealth he found his dream.
Bliss to the fingers of fishes who move about him
and to songs that rise like weeds from the hilly floor."
At this he coughed and finished off the bottle,
leaned it against the tub of the rubber-tree plant.

"I'd better not stay for your children, you know," he told me,
"but give them this and tell them it comes from you."
He slipped a bracelet of hair from his wrist and kissed it,
once for each wooden bead that held it fast.
"Look through this and the truth will not elude you.
Be faithful and it will raise the heaviest stone.
The morning star will sit in your bedroom window."
He put it in my hand and went out by the kitchen door.
When the children came, I was sitting where he left me
with the clumsy still-life of crackers, cheese, and milk.
They stopped in the doorway; I looked through the bracelet
and the white roots of their bones held up the air.

COUSIN ELLA GOES TO TEXAS

I reckon it was 19 and 52
and I was going to drive Bea and her kids
to Corpus Christi, Texas in my old Chev
and my brother Joe took a look at her and said
Eller, you going to slide right into Mexico on them tires.
So I went up to Frank Gergley's and said, Frank
I'm fixing to take Bea and her two out to Texas
and I need new tires. I didn't have much money
but he said Time would be fine.
Got his boy Oxie to unlug the old tires
then wrenched the new ones on hisself.
They weren't brand-new, but they had grit.

So I drove her home and we loaded her
and before the sun could slip its egg in the pan next morning
we was off. Bea's two, Rhonda and Mark, didn't even get
carsick till we hit the Smokies.
Well, we'd got the kids cleaned off
and was bearing down on Memphis
and Bea'd broke out the bologna sandwiches
when I heard it
first like a beaver slapping his tail:
k-twack, k-thwunk, k-thwack, k-thwunk.
What's that? Bea had a bite balled up

93

in the side of her mouth like a squirrel.
Well, it ain't the song of the open road, I told her.
I guess we better pull over and have her checked.

Man came out grinning. I said
I got something wrong with my tires. You check
the back ones after you fill her up. And he did.
Bea and the kids was hunting the Ladies
when he slunk around the side of the car.
Looks like your retreads is coming loose, Mayam,
he said, pouring it out like syrup. I like to knocked
his pitcher over getting out of that car.

What do you mean retreads? These is brand-new
secondhand tires. No Mayam, they's retreads
and the new tread's about to let go.

I could've boiled over like a radiator, I was
that mad -- at Frank and Bea and Texas and them tires
and dollars for not growing nowheres that you can get to--
but I just said Shoot and kicked one up front.
Only one in the bunch that kept its scalp.

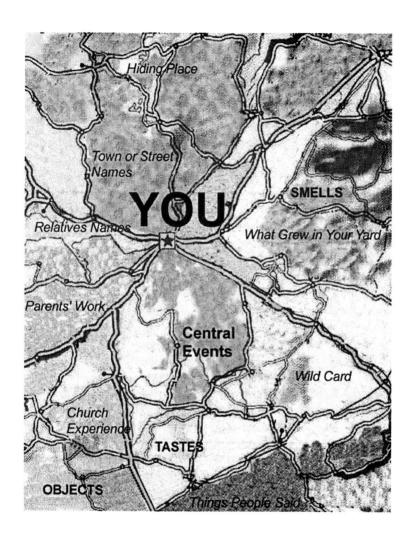

Hiding Place

Town or Street Names

YOU

SMELLS

Relatives Names

What Grew in Your Yard

Parents' Work

Central Events

Wild Card

Church Experience

TASTES

OBJECTS

Things People Said

where you're from

Now that you have traveled through this book, discovering things about yourself as well as about poetry, I have one last exercise to give you. Like those you have already tried, it can be done again and again.

Go back to the title poem and read it aloud. Those words won't fit you, of course, because the "I" of that poem is me, but the rhythm and images may stir memories of your own. Write them down. To lengthen your list, look at the categories included in the poem. They're on the map on the previous page. Try to come up with one or two items for each of them.

Let your list rest. Go do yoga or run cross-country or build a birdhouse. Then come back and read it with a fresh eye. How can you bring the reader closer? What if, instead of saying, "I'm from my grandmother's cooking," you said, "I'm from the corn fritters and spare ribs that my grandmother served up every Sunday of her life"? That's an exaggeration, of course; she probably didn't do it when she was a kid. And maybe your grandmother is a physicist and a vegetarian. Or maybe you have kosher deli take-out on Sunday. Whatever. Tell us about it. Tighten the focus on your original statements. Wake up your senses. Then think about the order.

You might arrange the images chronologically from least important to most important. (If you write individual sentences or phrases on Post-It Notes, they're easy to rearrange.) You might turn them into questions. As my friend, the poet Dick Hague, pointed out, you can reverse the whole thing and say where you're NOT from. However you go at it, play with order and rhythm including when to use "I'm from" and when to leave it out. Read your words aloud to see if they sing or hiss or create whatever effect it is you want.

If you don't like what you've got after this session, wait a day or two and do the exercise again. This time, try writing about where you're from right this minute. I could say, for example, "I'm from a big Target bill and a little bank balance." What places, people, songs, and foods define your life just now? Make the reader hear the screek of the metal curtain as it's raised at the mall store where you work. See the exact green of your nail polish. Taste your dreams.

Poems come from you: that's the secret. Give them all you've got. People will listen.

GROWING LIGHT

I write this poem
out of darkness
to you
who are also in darkness
because our lives demand it.

This poem is a hand on your shoulder
a bone touch to go with you
through the hard birth of vision.
In other words, love
shapes this poem
           is the fist that holds the chisel
           muscle that drags marble
           and burns with the weight
                  of believing a face
                  lives in the stone
                  a breathing word in the body.

I tell you
though the darkness
has been ours
words will give us
give our eyes, opened in promise
a growing light.

GEORGE ELLA LYON
SUMMER 1997

About the Photographer

Robert Hoskins was born in Harlan, Kentucky and educated at Yale University and the University of Kentucky. He is professor of English at James Madison University and is the author of *Graham Greene: A Character Index and Guide* (1991) and a forthcoming book is *Graham Greene: An Approach to the Novels*. His photographs have appeared in textbooks and college literary magazines.

"Where You're From" Map Design by Cathy Boyd